A AARON

A

MA

A

DAY S OO66 6

HAPPY FAAHER

THE SPACE SHUTTLE

A Photographic History

Philip S. Harrington

THE SPACE SHUTTLE

A Photographic History

PHILIP S. HARRINGTON

PHOTOGRAPHY BY
ROGER RESSMEYER/CORBIS AND OTHERS

BROWNTROUT PUBLISHERS

San Francisco

ISBN: 0-7631-7063-1
Printed in Korea

THE IMAGES ON TWO PREVIOUS PAGES:

***Discovery* at Sunset.** The space shuttle *Discovery* sits on Launch Pad 39-B on the eve of the launch of the twenty-sixth space shuttle mission (STS-26). Kennedy Space Center, Cape Canaveral, Florida. *September 28 1988.*
© Roger Ressmeyer/CORBIS

Powering Down Space Shuttle *Endeavour*. Commander Robert "Hoot" Gibson (left) and Pilot Curtis Brown power down space shuttle *Endeavour* after landing at 8:53 a.m. EDT on September 20, 1992, on Runway 33 of Kennedy Space Center. The international crew of STS-47 included the first Japanese astronaut to fly aboard the Shuttle, the first African-American woman to fly in space, and the first married couple to fly on the same space mission. © NASA/Roger Ressmeyer/CORBIS

THE SPACE SHUTTLE: A Photographic History

Philip S. Harrington

Columbus, Magellan, Lewis and Clark, Lindbergh. All of these pioneers faced great personal danger, yet each pressed on in the name of exploration and the betterment of humankind. Their herculean efforts affected not only their world, but also human civilization for all future generations.

Where have all the explorers gone? In fact, they are still very much with us, still pushing the limits of discovery. Some have taken the ultimate trip, leaving the safe haven of planet Earth and venturing out into the cosmos. They are the first generation to pursue a dream that has been in people's minds and souls since the dawn of history: the exploration of space. It's the stuff that dreams were made of. Yet today, we are privileged to live in an age when those dreams are starting to be realized.

Space Shuttle Blasting Off. Kennedy Space Center, Cape Canaveral, Florida. © NASA/Roger Ressmeyer/CORBIS

Each of the first space explorers, including USSR cosmonaut Yuri Gagarin and U.S. Mercury astronauts Alan Shepard and John Glenn, braved traveling into space alone inside cramped, life-sustaining capsules perched atop military missiles. Later, Gemini astronauts traveled in pairs, but even the three-person Apollo lunar missions in the late 1960s and early 1970s followed the same basic philosophy: expense was secondary to objective. To achieve the goal of landing on the Moon, astronauts were launched in small capsules on expendable rockets. Once the mission was over, none of the equipment could be used again on subsequent flights. Although this one-shot approach certainly met the objective of going to the Moon, the National Aeronautics and Space Administration realized that to continue a viable space program, they would need a less expensive, reusable rocket.

Even before Neil Armstrong and Edwin Aldrin landed on the Moon aboard *Apollo 11* in July 1969, NASA was imagining a reusable space plane that would become the backbone of our nation's space program in the coming decades. From the start, it was envisioned that the proposed "space shuttle" would launch vertically like a rocket, but land on a runway like a conventional aircraft. Plans were laid, objectives were set, and on January 5, 1972, President Richard Nixon announced the inception of the Space Shuttle Program.

The space shuttle, officially called the Space Transport System (STS), was to consist of something that looked like a stumpy-winged airplane (the orbiter) stuck on the back of a huge fuel tank straddled by a pair of missiles. The orbiter (commonly called the "shuttle" just by itself) was to be—at 148 feet long, 47 feet wide, and 74 tons tare—about the size of a DC-9 airplane. It was to be attached directly to a giant expendable tank filled with liquid hydrogen and oxygen fuel that would be used to feed the orbiter's three aft rocket engines. Two long and lean reusable solid-propellant rocket boosters were also to be strapped to the backbone of this towering external fuel tank. On the ground and fully fueled, the whole STS assemblage would weigh over two thousand tons. The whole thing would go up as a unit, its successive propulsion systems providing almost seven millions pounds of thrust.

The entire launch sequence would consist of almost innumerable steps that would take several days of checks and rechecks before final countdown could commence. Although the countdown clock would begin at "T minus 43 hours," there would be a number of built-in "holds" along the way—as when the external tank would be fueled up. On the last day of the countdown, the crew would enter the shuttle about three hours before the launch to perform final pre-launch checks of all systems in coordination with the ground crew. Ground and orbiter computers would continuously scan all data streaming in from some two thousand sensors and shut down the launch in milliseconds if anything were wrong.

Space Shuttle in Orbit. Cargo bay open.
© NASA/Roger Ressmeyer/CORBIS

The Ground Launch Sequencer, the mainframe computer controlling the final countdown since the last built-in hold at T minus 9 minutes, would "hand off" countdown control to the orbiter's onboard computers at T minus 31 seconds. "Ten … nine … eight … seven … six … we have main-engine start." At T minus 6.6 seconds, the shuttle's three aft main engines would have ignited, causing the shuttle to lean over slightly (or "twang"). "Four … three … two … one … and lift-off." At T minus zero, the solid rocket boosters would ignite; the explosive bolts that have kept the shuttle pinned to the ground for the last six seconds would blow off; and the shuttle would lift off the pad.

The solid rocket boosters would burn all 2.2 million pounds of their propellant in the first two minutes, providing seventy percent of thrust needed to hoist the STS twenty-eight miles above the surface of the Earth, almost to the roof of the stratosphere. There the boosters would separate, reach their forty-one-mile apogee a minute later, and then fall into the Atlantic Ocean 140 miles downrange of the Kennedy Space Center, to be recovered by ships and reused on subsequent missions. The orbiter's three rockets, consuming liquid fuel from the giant external fuel tank at the rate of three thousand pounds per second, would bring the orbiter almost to orbit about six-and-a-half minutes later. At that point the main engines would cut off. Forty-five minutes and half-an-orbit into the mission, the empty tank would be jettisoned to disintegrate and burn as it re-entered the atmosphere over the Indian Ocean. Now all alone, the orbiter would fire up two smaller rockets called its Orbital Maneuvering System in order to circularize its orbit at the selected altitude, between 120 and 240 miles.

Astronauts with "For Sale" Sign. Mission Specialist Dale Gardner, left, holds a "for sale" sign over the recovered Westar-VI satellite in the cargo bay of space shuttle *Discovery* during the fourteenth shuttle mission (51-A). Mission Specialist Joseph Allen hovers at the end of the remote manipulator system (RMS) arm, which cherry-picked the malfunctioning satellite from its excessively low orbit and deposited it in the shuttle's cargo bay. *November 14 1984.* © NASA/Roger Ressmeyer/CORBIS

Once in orbit, the crew would get down to its meticulously planned mission. Behind the crew compartment, which could hold up to seven members, a large cargo bay would release a wide variety of civilian and military payloads into Earth orbit. Each shuttle was to have a lifespan of one hundred space missions.

NASA engineers, as well as several aeronautical companies across the country, set out to design what would be the most sophisticated piece of equipment ever devised. It was clear from the start that the shuttle would be a completely new type of spacecraft, posing many unique engineering challenges. One of the first design problems encountered was how to bring the shuttle back to Earth safely. As a spacecraft returns to Earth, friction with our atmosphere heats the spacecraft to thousands of degrees, incinerating it instantly if left unprotected.

All of the earlier Mercury, Gemini, and Apollo missions used ablative heat shields designed to burn away during spacecraft re-entry, displacing the heat in the process. This approach was fine for one-time use, but a completely new approach would be needed for a reusable spacecraft. The solution came in the form of special ceramic tiles capable of withstanding temperatures over 18,000 degrees Fahrenheit. Twenty-four thousand of these ultra-light silica-fiber tiles affixed to the aluminum and graphite structural skin of the underbelly and wings of the shuttle would absorb the heat generated by friction during re-entry and insulate the shuttle with its precious human payload. The tiles would provide such efficient surface heat dissipation that an uncoated tile might be picked up with bare hands even while the interior of the tile was glowing red at 2,300 degrees Fahrenheit. No two tiles would have the same shape and each one would have to be precisely machined and painstakingly installed by hand so that it would flawlessly perform its thermal and aerodynamic functions for one hundred missions in temperatures ranging from minus 250 degrees Fahrenheit in space to 3,000 degrees Fahrenheit during re-entry.

Designers also had to devise a way to land the shuttle safely on dry land. Up until then, all American spacecraft had been retrieved by aircraft carriers after splashing down in the ocean. The shuttle was to land like a conventional aircraft—or, more correctly, like a glider … a glider traveling many times the speed of sound, that is! Auxiliary jet engines were ruled out early in the design, since they could not work in a space environment and would only add unnecessary weight to an already heavy vehicle. Instead, the shuttle's descent would be completely unpowered, leading one person to liken it to landing an aerodynamic rock. Onboard computer control would have to be very sophisticated, since there would be only one attempt at landing, with no chance to pull up and try again. After several proposals were received and studied, NASA awarded the prime contract to Rockwell International of Palmdale, California, in July 1972.

To test the shuttle's handling as it traveled through the atmosphere on approach and landing, NASA decided that Rockwell should build a test shuttle that would look and behave just like later shuttles except for one important difference: it couldn't fly into space. Instead, it would have to be carried high into Earth's atmosphere on top of a specially outfitted Boeing 747 jumbo jet and then released to plummet safely, it was hoped, back to the ground.

After taking more than four years to construct, the first shuttle rolled out of Rockwell's Air Force Plant 42, Site 1 assembly facility in September 1976. NASA originally planned to call it *Constitution*, but a massive write-in campaign by fans of the *Star Trek* television series convinced officials to christen it *Enterprise*. No matter the name, one look and everyone knew they were witnessing the dawn of a new and exciting age of space exploration. Gone were the tiny capsules. They had been relegated to history forever, replaced by a sleek and smooth space plane that looked to be right out of a science fiction story. But this was *real*!

Nine months of grueling approach-and-landing tests at Edwards Air Force Base began in February 1977. Each time, *Enterprise* was lofted to an altitude ranging between 19,000 and 26,000 feet and released. Each time, she glided back gracefully and safely to Edwards. Although these tests uncovered several key problems that were subsequently corrected in the four orbiters built to go into Earth orbit, they had demonstrated that the shuttle worked!

Space Shuttle *Atlantis* over the Strait of Gibraltar. The nose of the space shuttle *Atlantis* over the Strait of Gibraltar, as seen from the *Mir* space station while docked with *Atlantis*.
Digital image © 1996 CORBIS; Original image courtesy of NASA/CORBIS

Construction of the first space-ready space shuttle began in March 1975 and took almost four years to complete. With great anticipation, it was rolled out on March 8, 1979, and christened *Columbia*, after the first American ship to circumnavigate the globe. *Columbia* would undergo another two years of ground-based tests before rocketing away from Pad 39-A at the Kennedy Space Center in Florida at 7:00 A. M. eastern time on April 12, 1981. Dubbed STS-1, the mission took astronauts Commander John Young and Pilot Robert Crippen into Earth orbit to test *Columbia*'s spaceworthiness. When they safely landed at Edwards two days later, they had proven that the shuttle could work well in the frigid vacuum of space and then survive the scorching heat of re-entry through our atmosphere. The main operational phase of the Space Shuttle Program was now underway.

Rockwell began constructing a third space shuttle—*Challenger*—in June 1975. Although originally intended to be a test model like *Enterprise, Challenger* was subsequently retrofitted to become the nation's second fully functional orbital vehicle. Named after a U.S. hydrological research vessel that explored the Atlantic and Pacific Oceans during the 1870s, *Challenger* was completed in June 1982 and saw its maiden launch the following April 4.

With the success of *Columbia* and *Challenger*, NASA ordered two more shuttles from Rockwell. The third

Space Shuttle and Light Phenomenon.
© NASA/Roger Ressmeyer/CORBIS

flight-ready shuttle, *Discovery*, was named after one of the two ships used by the British explorer Captain James Cook for his third Pacific voyage, which ended fatally for him with his discovery in 1779 of the Hawaiian Islands. *Discovery*'s construction was finished in October 1983, with its inaugural lift-off on August 30, 1984. The fourth shuttle, *Atlantis*, was named after the primary research vessel of the Woods Hole Oceanographic Institute in Massachusetts from 1930 to 1966. *Atlantis* was completed in March 1985 and saw its inaugural voyage on October 3 that same year. Just like their sister ships *Columbia* and *Challenger*, *Discovery* and *Atlantis* proved to be amazing feats of engineering.

With a fleet of four operational shuttles, NASA began an ambitious program that called for no less than one launch per month. Beginning with the second mission, abbreviated STS-2, satellites have been regularly carried into Earth orbit by the shuttles. Using the shuttle's Canadian-made articulated arm (Canadarm), astronauts gently lift the cargo from the bay and release it into space. Many unique instruments and cameras have also been carried in the cargo bay to collect data and take measurements from orbit. In 1984, for instance, in addition to their primary payloads, shuttle missions 41-C, 41-D, and 41-G each carried a wide-format IMAX movie camera to generate the footage for the documentary film, *The Dream is Alive*.

From the start, the Space Shuttle Program was intended to open the universe to a wider array of astronauts than ever before. Previously, U.S. astronauts were always male and almost always military test pilots. But with the shuttle came the opportunity for many others to join the elite ranks of the astronaut corps. *Challenger*'s second flight in June 1983, for instance, saw America's first female astronaut, Mission Specialist Sally Ride, as a member of the STS-7 crew. Dr. Ride later flew a second time on board *Challenger* as part of mission 41-G in 1984, joined by Kathryn Sullivan, America's second female astronaut. Mission Specialist Guion Bluford became the first African-American astronaut on the following shuttle mission, STS-8, when *Challenger* rocketed a crew of five into orbit in August 1983. German Ulf Merbold, the first non-American to fly into space aboard the shuttle, was a member of *Columbia*'s STS-9 crew. Later missions would carry crewmembers from Argentina, Brazil, Canada, France, India, Israel, Italy, Japan, Russia, Saudi Arabia, Sweden, and Switzerland. The shuttle proved that space belonged to all of mankind, not just an elite few.

Shuttle *Atlantis* at Space Station. © NASA/Roger Ressmeyer/CORBIS

Unlike the earlier capsules, which were just large enough to hold the astronauts and some basic carry-on equipment, the shuttle's versatile design was spacious enough to perform many different types of work in space. For instance, the STS-9 mission marked the first time that Spacelab was carried in the shuttle's cargo bay. A joint venture between NASA and the European Space Agency, Spacelab was an orbital laboratory where many unique experiments could be performed beyond the bounds of Earth's gravity. Scientific research conducted on this and other science missions may have seemed out of this world to some, but their results produced many down-to-Earth benefits, including advances in medicine, microminiaturization, chemistry, materials science, meteorology, and many other scientific disciplines.

The first mission of 1984, designated 41-B, saw another program milestone when astronauts Bruce McCandless and Robert Stewart took the first untethered spacewalks using nitrogen thruster-powered backpacks called manned maneuvering units, or MMUs. Up to that point, all spacewalks (or "extra-vehicular activities," as they are sometimes called) had required an umbilical lifeline to the spacecraft. Each MMU, by contrast, had its own integral maneuvering thrusters, air and fluid packs, and air conditioners. Once the astronauts suited up in their MMUs and stepped away from the shuttle, each became a human satellite. Imagine the freedom to fly over Earth's clouds and oceans in your own, personally tailored spaceship!

Shuttle flights continued, but postponements due to inclement weather and, more often, faulty equipment plagued NASA's ambitious schedule. Although twenty-four successful launches took place between April 1981 and January 1986, many were delayed, some by as much as a month. Ridicule in the press further embarrassed NASA and increased public discontent.

One way that NASA hoped to recapture the magic of its earlier manned programs was to launch a private citizen into space. On August 27, 1984, President Ronald Reagan announced that a teacher would be the first private citizen to fly on the space shuttle. A nationwide search was conducted, with applications received from more than eleven thousand teachers. After exhaustive interviews, NASA announced their candidate: Christa McAuliffe, a social studies teacher from Concord High School in Concord, New Hampshire. She was perfect in every way, a wholesome, well-spoken, exuberant individual who immediately captured the hearts and imagination of the nation. When asked why their teacher should be chosen over the other candidates, McAuliffe's students answered that she was an "inspirational human being, a marvelous teacher who made their lessons come alive."

Astronaut Floating outside Space Shuttle.
© Roger Ressmeyer/CORBIS

The twenty-fifth shuttle mission, designated 51-L and using *Challenger*, was chosen as the Teacher-in-Space mission. Chronic problems persisted. Uncooperative weather and equipment difficulties repeatedly pushed back the original launch date of January 22, 1986. After several postponements, the launch was scheduled again for January 28. Another scrub seemed inevitable, however, when the temperature fell below freezing overnight. Since NASA had never launched a shuttle at a temperature less than 50 degrees Fahrenheit, engineers voiced concern over possible performance problems. How would the shuttle's almost uncountable launch systems behave in the cold? Most had expected another postponement, but NASA management continued the countdown. Even though sections of the launch pad were covered in ice, and despite a frigid temperature of 36 degrees Fahrenheit at the time of launch, *Challenger* finally lifted off from Pad 39-B at the Kennedy Space Center at 11:38 a.m. eastern time.

Although the lift-off appeared to be normal at the time, with *Challenger* roaring into a cloudless sky, the seven astronauts onboard were destined never to reach orbit. Instead, as they left the bounds of their home planet, they were rocketing into immortality. Fifty-two seconds into the mission, after clearing the atmospheric zone of maximum density, the shuttle's main engines automatically throttled up to their full "104-percent" thrust (namely, 104 percent of the main engines' power rating in original STS design standard set in 1972, which was exceeded by nine per cent in the engines that were actually built by Rocketdyne). Seventy-three seconds after lift-off, the unimaginable happened: *Challenger* exploded. All seven astronauts aboard—Commander Francis (Dick) Scobee; Pilot Michael Smith; Mission Specialists Judith Resnik, Ellison Onizuka, and

Ronald McNair; and Payload Specialists Gregory Jarvis and Christa McAuliffe—were killed.

What could have possibly triggered such a terrible accident? That was the charge given to an accident investigation team appointed by President Reagan. They looked at every aspect of the shuttle, reviewing film of the doomed launch over and over again, studying every section of the complex spacecraft. At launch, *Challenger* was made up of the four separate components described above: the orbiter itself, the main fuel tank, and the pair of solid-propellant rocket boosters. Each of the boosters was built like a stack of tin cans, with one section fitted precisely to the next. In order to keep the fuel that was burning inside the booster from escaping through one of the overlapping joints, each junction was sealed with zinc chromate putty and two high-temperature O-rings that measured 37 feet long and 0.25 inch thick.

External Fuel Tank Falling from Space Shuttle. The external fuel tank of the space shuttle falls toward the Indian Ocean after separating from the space shuttle. *© NASA/Roger Ressmeyer/CORBIS*

Professor Richard Feyman, a member of the presidential commission, found that, although the O-rings maintained a tight seal at high temperature, they lost their resiliency as the temperature dropped toward freezing. As a result, the O-rings compressed under the great force of the joint overnight, but never sprang back to form a good seal prior to launch due to the cold temperature. Propellant burned through the weakened joint, eventually triggering an explosion of the main fuel tank, destroying *Challenger*.

The nation, indeed the entire world, was stunned by the loss. At a national memorial service held on January 31 at Houston's Johnson Space Center, President Reagan eulogized the seven fallen *Challenger* astronauts in a moving speech that concluded:

> Your families and your country mourn your passing. We bid you goodbye. We will never forget you. For those who knew you well and loved you, the pain will be deep and enduring. A nation, too, will long feel the loss of her seven sons and daughters, her seven good friends. We can find consolation only in faith, for we know in our hearts that you who flew so high and so proud now make your home beyond the stars, safe in God's promise of eternal life.

The shuttle program was suspended for more than two years until the investigation into the *Challenger* disaster was complete and a solution was put in place to ensure that a similar accident would never happen again. When shuttle *Discovery* lifted off on September 29, 1988, it did so with completely redesigned solid rocket boosters as well as hundreds of other safety improvements—and a new philosophy at NASA that perhaps space flight wasn't meant to be so routine after all.

To replace the ill-fated *Challenger*, NASA awarded a new contract to Rockwell to build a new shuttle. That shuttle, christened *Endeavour* after the ship commanded by Captain James Cook on his first Pacific voyage (1768-1771), was completed in April 1991. *Endeavour*'s first flight occurred as mission STS-49, launched on May 7, 1992.

Although problems continued to crop up in the shuttle program even after *Challenger*'s destruction, there were many more moments of success. One of the crowning moments was the release into Earth orbit of the Hubble Space Telescope from *Discovery*'s cargo bay on mission STS-31 in April 1990. With its watchful eye above Earth's obscuring atmosphere, the long-awaited Hubble held the promise of being the single greatest leap ever in our probing of the universe.

Although the shuttle and its crew executed their job flawlessly, subsequent tests showed that the Hubble's eye was myopic due to faulty construction. A remedy took more than three years to concoct. In December 1993, shuttle mission STS-61 returned to the Hubble telescope. Five valiant spacewalks from the shuttle *Endeavour* were needed to install new corrective equipment. By the time the astronauts returned to Earth eleven days later, Hubble was functioning perfectly. Since then, Hubble has been an unqualified success, providing the deepest views of the universe yet made in the visible spectrum, to within one billion years of the Big Bang. To this day, Hubble continues to discover new sights and solve old mysteries, such as the rate of expansion of the universe.

Space Shuttle *Columbia* on Launch Pad at Night. Floodlights bathe the *Columbia*, the first of America's space shuttles, the night before its first launch. Kennedy Space Center, Cape Canaveral, Florida. *April 12 1981.* © Roger Ressmeyer/CORBIS

In addition to the Hubble Space Telescope, many other communications, weather, scientific, and military satellites have also been ferried into Earth orbit by the shuttles. In 1989, shuttle mission STS-34 launched the highly successful *Galileo* unmanned spacecraft toward Jupiter from the *Atlantis* cargo bay. Ten years later, the 1999 deployment of the orbiting Chandra X-Ray Observatory from *Columbia* on STS-93 opened up another new window on the cosmos. In tandem with the Hubble telescope, Chandra gives astronomers unprecedented views of high-energy objects in the universe, such as exploding stars and colliding galaxies.

The shuttle has also served as a wonderful vehicle for advancing diplomacy, signaling the start of a new era of international cooperation in space. What was considered impossible only a few years earlier became a post-Cold War reality in 1994, when the United States teamed up with its former rival Russia on several shuttle missions. That year, Sergei Krikalev became the first Russian cosmonaut to travel on the shuttle, when he became a member of the STS-60 crew. A year later on STS-63, *Discovery* traveled to within thirty-seven feet of the Russian *Mir* space station in a dress rehearsal for the STS-71 mission.

The June 1995 launch of STS-71 marked the one-hundredth U.S. human space launch, as well as the first time a shuttle docked with the Russian space station *Mir*. After a short welcoming ceremony, joint operations included scientific investigations in the shuttle's Spacelab module. Along with supplies, *Atlantis* transported a new two-member crew to *Mir* and returned the three who had staffed the station for the past several months. Those coming back from their tour of duty included American astronaut Norman Thagard, who had been launched to *Mir* earlier on a Russian Soyuz TM-21 rocket.

STS-71 was the first of nine shuttle missions to *Mir*. As part of the March 1996 STS-76 mission, *Atlantis* returned to *Mir* with Shannon Lucid, the first American woman to live on the space station. She would spend the next 188 days in Earth orbit, finally returning to Earth on board *Atlantis* with the crew of STS-79.

Lucid's joining the *Mir* crew also began a continuous U.S. presence on *Mir* that would last for the next two years. That presence was not without its dangers, however. Troubles began shortly after *Atlantis* had swapped Lucid for astronaut Jerry Linenger on STS-81 in January 1997. Over the course of the next four months, Linenger and his Russian crew mates faced many challenges, including battling the most severe fire ever aboard an orbiting spacecraft as well as repairing numerous failures of critical onboard systems.

Troubles continued for astronaut Michael Foale,

Space Shuttle *Columbia* on Launch Pad at Dawn. *Columbia*, the first of America's space shuttles, sits at Launch Pad 39A on the morning of its first launch. Kennedy Space Center, Cape Canaveral, Florida. *April 12 1981.* © Roger Ressmeyer/CORBIS

Linenger's replacement, who joined *Mir* from *Atlantis* on mission STS-84 in May 1997. On June 25, an unmanned Russian resupply ship collided with *Mir*'s experiment-housing Spektr module, ripping a hole in the station and causing depressurization. Although much of Foale's scientific work conducted in the Spektr module was lost, *Mir*'s modular design let the crew seal off the damaged section quickly. Fortunately, food, water, and other critical needs were stored in other modules, which were undamaged.

By welcome contrast, later missions to *Mir*, including the September 1997 STS-86 launch of *Atlantis* and January 1998 STS-89 launch of *Endeavour*, were largely uneventful. The continual failures had proved, however, that *Mir* had outlived its useful life. After all, portions of the space station had been in orbit since 1986. As a result of increasing safety concerns, the June 1998 STS-91 mission of *Discovery* marked the end of the Shuttle-Mir project. *Mir* was finally de-orbited on March 23, 2001, re-entering Earth's atmosphere near Fiji and falling harmlessly into the South Pacific.

The October 1998 launch of *Discovery* mission STS-95 had onboard as one of its crew a notable figure in American history. John Glenn, one of the seven original Mercury astronauts and the first American to orbit Earth, was returning to space after 36 years. Payload Specialist Glenn, then 77, endured a battery of medical tests conducted in another onboard laboratory module called SpaceHab, which was installed in the cargo bay. These tests furthered research in how the absence of gravity affects balance, metabolism, and other aspects of human physiology in older individuals. Glenn's response to the tests was amazing, proving that he still had "the right stuff."

Since 1998, most shuttle missions have been focused on constructing the largest international cooperative space venture in history: the International Space Station, or ISS. Assembly began on STS-88 in December 1998, when the *Endeavour* crew rendezvoused with the station's Zarya Control Module. The first piece of the ISS to be put into orbit, Zarya had been launched by an unmanned Russian rocket a month earlier. The *Endeavour* crew mated Zarya to an American-made passageway module called the Unity Node, which they had carried up in the shuttle's cargo bay.

Space Shuttle *Columbia* Lifting Off. *Columbia*, the first of America's space shuttles, lifts off at 7 a.m. EST, April 12, 1981, on the inaugural space shuttle mission, STS-1. Kennedy Space Center, Cape Canaveral, Florida. © *Roger Ressmeyer/CORBIS*

STS-88 was the first of more than forty flights from the United States and Russia that will be needed to complete construction of the International Space Station. Its modular design, however, has allowed expeditions to live on board the station since November 2000. The first team—Commander William Shepherd, Soyuz Pilot Yuri Gidzenko, and Flight Engineer Sergei Krikalev—was launched to the ISS on board a Russian Soyuz spacecraft. They remained on the infant station for four months, when *Discovery*

mission STS-102 brought in members of Expedition Two. Crews of three continue to rotate on and off the ISS approximately once every six months, with interim shuttle missions continuing to resupply the station and build on mankind's dream of establishing a permanent residence in space. (You might even be able to spot the ISS yourself as it passes silently through the starry sky at night. Check the Web site www.heavens-above.com for predicted dates and times of passages.)

Although the focus of the Space Shuttle Program for the past several years has been the construction of the International Space Station, other missions have continued the program's original scientific work. Not outfitted to visit the ISS, *Columbia* continued to launch and maintain satellites (including the release of the Chandra X-ray Observatory and the servicing of the Hubble Space Telescope) and to serve as a platform for conducting microgravity experiments.

This, in fact, was the primary goal for STS-107, for which *Columbia* was launched from KSC Pad 39-A at 10:39 a.m. eastern time on January 16, 2003. *Columbia* was returning to orbit on its twenty-eighth mission after spending a year-and-a-half being retrofitted with the latest equipment and safety upgrades. Over the course of the next sixteen days and 255 orbits at an altitude of 170 miles, the emphasis would be on the work inside the SpaceHab research module within *Columbia*'s cargo bay. Crew members Lt. Col. Michael Anderson (Payload

Commander), Capt. David Brown (Mission Specialist), Dr. Laurel Clark (Physician Commander), Dr. Kalpana Chawla (Engineer) from India, and first-time Israeli astronaut Ilan Ramon (Payload Specialist) would perform over one hundred experiments in biology, medicine, and physical sciences; while Commander Col. Rick Husband and Pilot Commander William McCool tended to spacecraft operation on the flight deck.

When asked during the mission what her most thrilling moment was to that point, Dr. Chawla recalled a chance moment on the orbiter's flight deck. As the sun set, she could see her own reflection in the overhead windows, along with the sunlit and night sides of the Earth. "In the retina of my eye, the whole Earth and the sky could be seen reflected. I called all the crew members one by one, and they saw it, and everybody said, 'Oh, wow!'"

When asked the same question, first-time astronaut Dr. Clark mentioned how she had marveled at a student experiment that she was conducting. Clark watched as a newly hatched moth "was just starting to puff its wings up so that it would be able to fly." She was struck by the thought that "life continues in lots of places, and life is a magical thing."

Indeed, results from all experiments appeared to be very encouraging. As the mission was winding down,

Space Shuttle *Columbia* Landing. Accompanied by a chase plane, space shuttle *Columbia* comes in for landing at 10:20 a.m. PST, April 14, 1981, to end the 56-hour-long inaugural space shuttle mission, STS-1. Edwards Air Force Base, California.
© Roger Ressmeyer/CORBIS

Entry Flight Director Leroy Cain said: "This has been a very successful mission. It's far exceeded folks' expectations from a science standpoint, so we're very pleased. We had no problems. The vehicle performed flawlessly today, as it has the entire mission."

His exuberance, however, would soon turn to dismay. At 8:15 a.m. eastern time on February 1, 2003, *Columbia* initiated the de-orbit burn for her planned landing at Kennedy Space Center exactly one hour later. At 8:59 a.m. eastern time, only seventeen minutes from home, something went terribly wrong.

The first hint of a problem occurred at 8:52 a.m. eastern time, twenty-four minutes before the projected landing time. The spacecraft was forty-two miles above the Pacific Ocean, four hundred miles off the coast of California, enduring the intense heat of re-entry as it sledded into the upper atmosphere at twenty-one times the speed of sound (Mach 21). During that fateful minute, Mission Control reported that three sensors in the left wheel well registered abnormal temperature increases and four sensors near the back of the shuttle's left wing went off-line. As the shuttle hurtled onward over the next five minutes, five other sensors on *Columbia*'s left side recorded abnormal temperature increases. Just before 8:58 a.m. eastern time, while *Columbia* was over New Mexico, sensors indicated an increase in drag on the shuttle's left side and automatic compensations of the spacecraft's attitude by the flight control systems.

Less than eighteen minutes from home, while *Columbia* was descending over northern Texas at an altitude of 39 miles and moving at 12,500 miles per hour (Mach 18), the main landing gear left tire pressure sensors went off-line. Moments later, temperatures inside the left wheel well dropped abruptly. The tire pressure events caused an onboard alert and Commander Husband initiated a conversation about them with Mission Control. But the conversation was cut off. All crew communications and data telemetry from *Columbia* were intensely garbled for thirty-two seconds. At 8:59 A.M, they ceased.

During the same interval of time, skywatchers in the southwestern United States, who had been alerted to watch for *Columbia*'s fiery re-entry, gazed into the early morning sky. Just as promised, they saw *Columbia* streak across the sky, looking like a brilliant shooting star leaving a broad contrail in its wake. But there was something wrong. A sonic rumble was splitting the air over East Texas. And instead of a single streak, there were multiple trails. Mission Control, still frantically trying to restore lost communications, received the report from a television station that numerous pieces of the craft were visible spinning across the morning sky.

Space Shuttle *Challenger*. The newly completed space shuttle *Challenger* as seen from below and behind. Palmdale, California. *July 1982.* © Roger Ressmeyer/CORBIS

Although the physical cause of the catastrophe was (and, at time of writing, remains) a mystery, its tragic finality was at once clear to all the world. *Columbia* and her crew had perished in a fireball high over the Dallas-Fort Worth area. The mighty matriarch of the shuttle fleet and the seven extraordinary individuals who made up her crew were no more. Her wreckage lay spewed in a vast and desolate plume starting forty miles southwest of Fort Worth and crossing East Texas into western Louisiana.

To try and understand what caused the disaster, NASA immediately issued a plea to all citizens living in neighborhood of the debris field for help in locating and safeguarding the remains of *Columbia* and her crew. Within a week, more than twelve thousand fragments had been recovered, allowing NASA's internal investigation team and an independent review board (the Columbia Accident Investigation Board, under the chairmanship of Retired Navy Admiral Harold W. Gehman Jr.) to set about the mournful and arduous task of once again reconstructing an exploded shuttle to try to pinpoint exactly what went wrong.

Initial results of "reverse-engineering" the pattern of temperature spikes and sensor failures point to a small-hole breach of the aluminum skin somewhere on *Columbia*'s left side as the proximate cause of the disaster. The hole might have been on the surface of the left wing, on its leading edge, through the seal or door of the left wheel well, or in the fuselage. With the thermal insulation provided by the tiles somehow compromised at that point, the inferred hole is thought to have admitted a jet of plasma: the envelope of gas superheated to 3,000 degrees Fahrenheit that is generated against the thermal armor of the shuttle by the atmospheric friction of re-entry. The plasma flowed into the left wing and in quick succession triggered or cut the sensors in its path. And it played like a superhot blowtorch on the aluminum girders of the wing's inner frame, slicing through them like butter.

Still undetermined at time of writing is the ultimate cause of the breach to the thermal protection of the wing. What damaged the tiles enough to admit "burn-through"? What kind of impact might even have gashed the aluminum skin? Was it the two-foot-square, 2.7-pound chunk of hardened foam insulation that tracking cameras captured popping off the external fuel tank 81 seconds after lift-off and striking the leading edge of the orbiter's left wing near the fuselage? That was the theory tentatively advanced by Space Shuttle Program Manager Ron Dittemore in the immediate aftermath of the event. Or was it a collision while in orbit with a small meteoroid or a piece of space junk, as suggested by military radar detection of an unidentified object receding from *Columbia* a day after the launch? Or was it an electrical discharge in space from a solar storm? Only time will tell if we will ever know the answer for a certainty.

What is it about space that calls us to leave our fragile home world and go forth on the ultimate adventure? It's the same call that beckoned past explorers to the summit of Mount Everest or to the depths of the ocean floor. Human beings have a natural curiosity and an urge to explore the unknown. Countless generations could only dream about the ultimate adventure, the exploration of space. Today, we are living their dream. Perhaps President George W. Bush summed it up best in his eulogy of the "Columbia Seven" at the national memorial service on February 4, 2003:

> To leave behind Earth and air and gravity is an ancient dream of humanity. For these seven, it was a dream fulfilled. Each of these astronauts had the daring and discipline required of their calling. Each of them knew that great endeavors are inseparable from great risks. And each of them accepted those risks willingly, even joyfully, in the cause of discovery.

The cause of the *Columbia* disaster will probably be found, just as *Challenger*'s was, and the Space Shuttle Program will go on, better and safer than before. NASA will press on as well, both in the memory of its fallen family members as well as for the betterment of humankind and the quest for discovery. The need to explore the unknown is the very cornerstone of civilization. The same spirit that drove Columbus also drives our astronauts. Through their bravery, we have just begun to tiptoe into the vast ocean of the universe. We have not even gotten ankle-deep, yet the urge to continue out into deeper water is undeniable.

The Earth was created from a cloud of interstellar gas and dust over four billion years ago. Everything we know, everything we see, and everyone who has ever lived is made from material that was first formed inside ancient stars billions of years ago. Perhaps that is why our drive to explore space is so strong, for in a sense, each of our astronauts is leading our way home.

Rollout of Space Shuttle *Challenger*. A truck tows the newly completed space shuttle *Challenger* from its Palmdale construction facility to Edwards Air Force Base. Palmdale, California. *July 1982.*
© *Roger Ressmeyer/CORBIS*

Space Shuttle *Challenger* Riding on 747. The space shuttle *Challenger* is transported "piggy-back" on a NASA Boeing 747 from Edwards Air Force Base in California to Kennedy Space Center in Florida. Edwards Air Force Base, California. *July 4 1982.*

© *Roger Ressmeyer/CORBIS*

Space Shuttle Deploying Satellite. Artistic
visualization. © Roger Ressmeyer/CORBIS

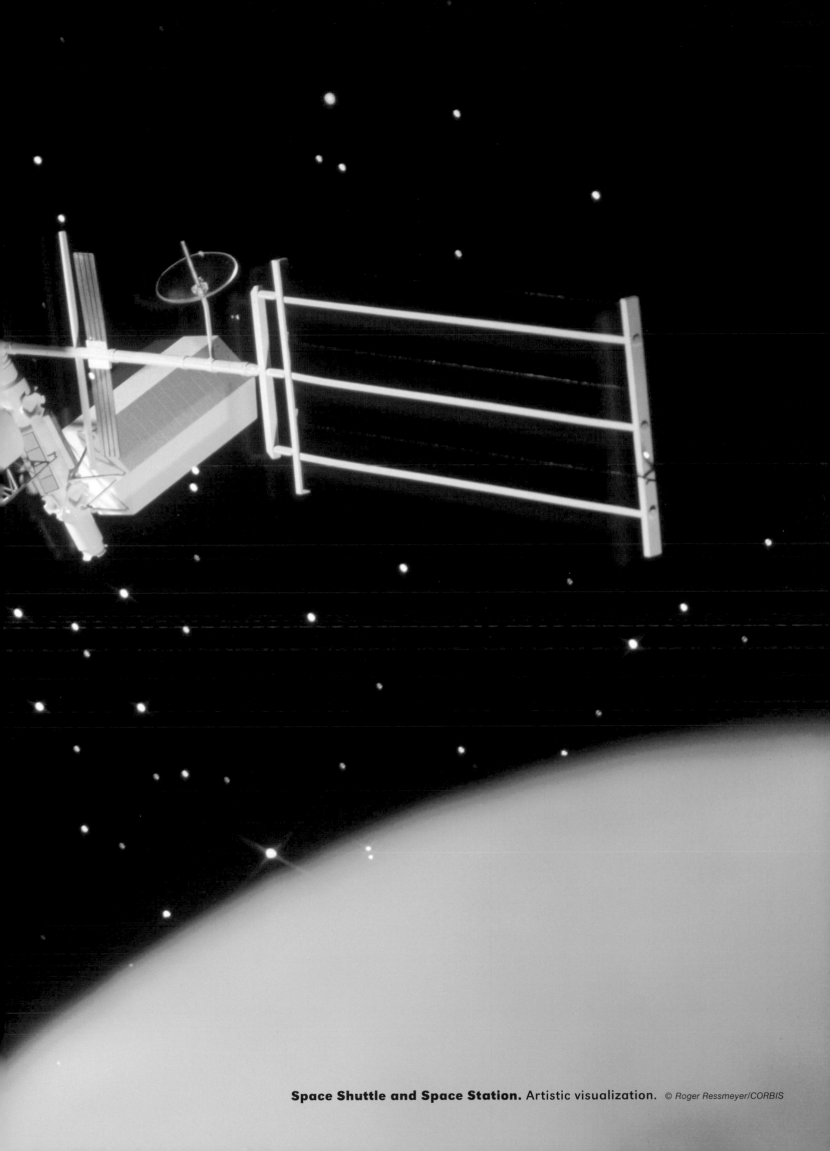

Space Shuttle and Space Station. Artistic visualization.   © Roger Ressmeyer/CORBIS

First Night Launch of the Space Shuttle. The space shuttle *Challenger* lifting off from Launch Pad 39-A at 2:32 a.m. EDT on August 29, 1983, for STS-8: the space shuttle's first night launch and the first space flight to carry an African-American astronaut (Guion Bluford). Kennedy Space Center, Cape Canaveral, Florida.

Sunrise from Orbit. Sunrise viewed over the tail of space shuttle *Columbia* during STS-9. *November 1983.* © NASA/Roger Ressmeyer/CORBIS

Space Shuttle *Columbia* Launching. The space shuttle *Columbia* blasting off at 11:00 a.m. EST on November 29, 1983, for STS-9: the space shuttle's first Spacelab mission and the first space flight to carry an astronaut representing the European Space Agency (Ulf Merbold of Germany). Kennedy Space Center, Cape Canaveral, Florida. © Roger Ressmeyer/CORBIS

Space Shuttle *Challenger* Launching. The space shuttle *Challenger* blasting off at 8:00 a.m. EST on February 3, 1984, for the tenth shuttle mission (41-B): the first space shuttle mission to land at Kennedy Space Center and the first to feature untethered spacewalks (by McCandless and Stewart). **Kennedy Space Center, Cape Canaveral, Florida.** © Museum of Flight/CORBIS

First Untethered Spacewalk. During the tenth space shuttle mission (41-B), Mission Specialist Bruce McCandless II ventures from shuttle *Challenger* on the first spacewalk using a manned maneuvering unit (MMU). *February 1984.*

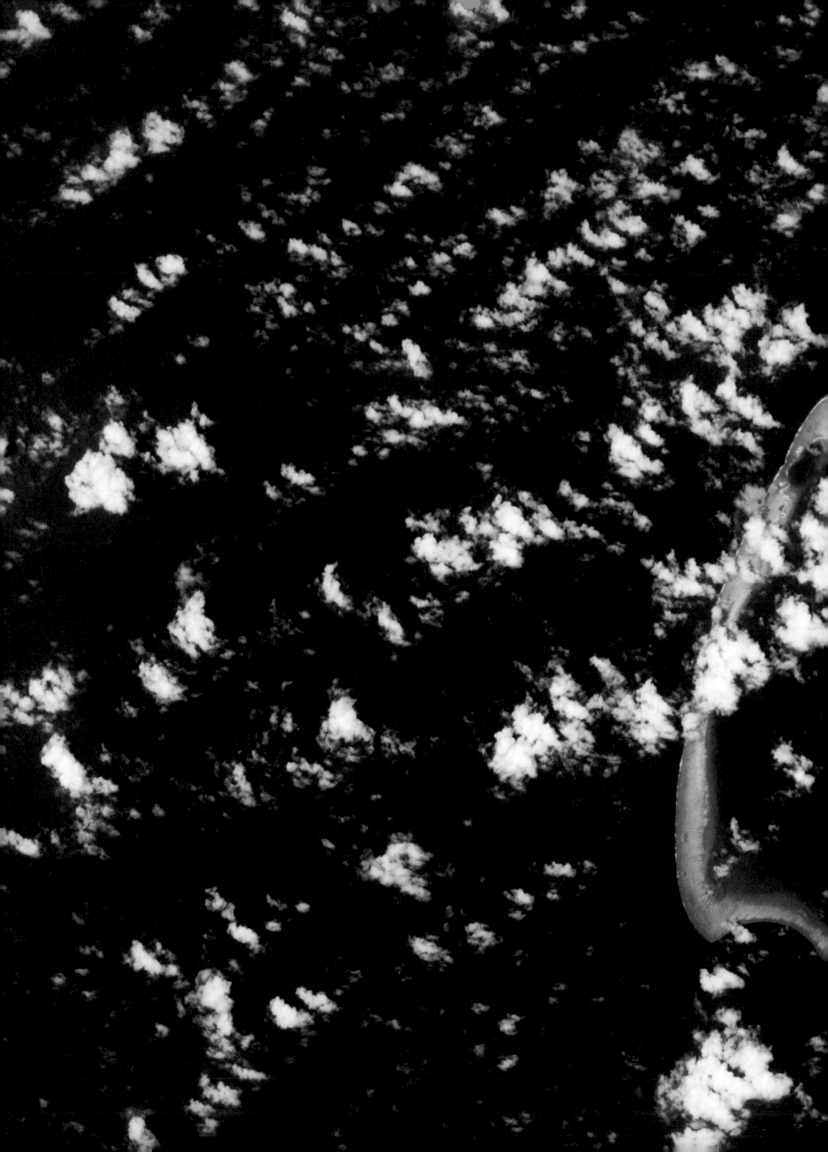

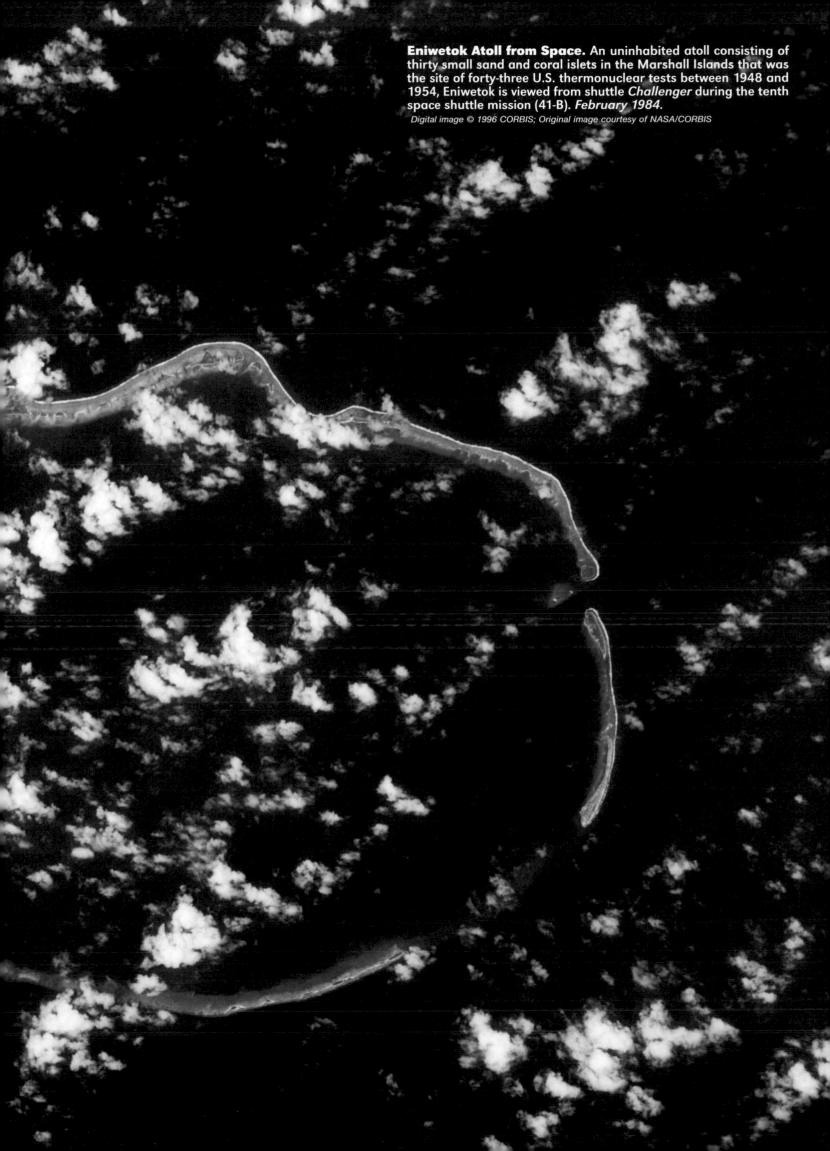

Eniwetok Atoll from Space. An uninhabited atoll consisting of thirty small sand and coral islets in the Marshall Islands that was the site of forty-three U.S. thermonuclear tests between 1948 and 1954, Eniwetok is viewed from shuttle *Challenger* during the tenth space shuttle mission (41-B). *February 1984.*

Astronaut in Cargo Bay of Shuttle *Challenger*. Astronaut with manned maneuvering unit (MMU) in cargo bay of shuttle *Challenger* during the eleventh shuttle mission (41-C). *April 6 1984.* © NASA/Roger Ressmeyer/CORBIS

Astronauts Repairing Satellite in Cargo Bay of Shuttle *Challenger*. Two astronauts in cargo bay of shuttle *Challenger* replace the altitude control system and coronagraph/polarimeter electronics box in the Solar Max satellite during the eleventh shuttle mission (41-C). *April 1984.* © NASA/Roger Ressmeyer/CORBIS

Space Shuttle *Challenger* Blasting Off. *Challenger* blasts off at 12:02 p.m. EDT on April 29, 1985, on the seventeenth shuttle mission (51-B). Kennedy Space Center, Cape Canaveral, Florida. *© CORBIS*

Space Shuttle over Strait of Hormuz. © CORBIS

Crew of Space Shuttle *Challenger*. The seven members of the twenty-fifth shuttle mission (51-L) included: (left to right, front row) Pilot Michael Smith, Commander Francis Scobee, and Mission Specialist Ronald McNair; (left to right, back row) Mission Specialist Ellison Onizuka, Payload Specialist Sharon Christa McAuliffe, Mission Specialist Gregory Jarvis, and Mission Specialist Judith Resnik. The crew lost their lives when the *Challenger* exploded 73 seconds after lift-off on January 28, 1986. *November 1985.*
© CORBIS

Space Shuttle *Challenger* Launching. The space shuttle *Challenger* lifting off from Launch Pad 39-B at 11:38 a.m. EST on January 28, 1986, for the twenty-fifth space shuttle mission (51-L): the first space flight to carry a civilian (teacher Christa McAuliffe). A minute later, the space shuttle exploded. Kennedy Space Center, Cape Canaveral, Florida. © CORBIS

Space Shuttle *Discovery* on Mobile Launch Pad. The space shuttle *Discovery* mounted on the mobile launch pad while being moved to Launch Pad 39-B for the twenty-sixth shuttle mission (STS-26), which would launch on September 29, 1988. *July 4 1988.* Kennedy Space Center, Cape Canaveral, Florida. © CORBIS

Space Shuttle *Discovery* on Launch Pad. The space shuttle *Discovery* sits on Launch Pad 39-B the night before its launch at 11:37 a.m. EDT on September 29, 1988, for the twenty-sixth shuttle mission (STS-26): the first since the Challenger disaster. Kennedy Space Center, Cape Canaveral, Florida.

Space Shuttle *Discovery* Bathed in Floodlights. The space shuttle *Discovery* sits on Launch Pad 39-B the night before its launch at 11:37 a.m. EDT on September 29, 1988, for the twenty-sixth shuttle mission (STS-26): the first since the *Challenger* disaster. Kennedy Space Center, Cape Canaveral, Florida. © *Roger Ressmeyer/CORBIS*

Space Shuttle *Discovery* Launching. The space shuttle *Discovery* rises from the pad at 11:37 a.m. EDT on September 29, 1988. The columns of white "smoke" obscuring the launch complex are actually composed of steam from the millions of gallons of water released from tanks on the launch pad just prior to ignition in order to control the heat of combustion of the fuel. Brown smoke and yellow flames shoot out of the two boosters (SRBs). The rocket flames are reflected in the water. Birds disturbed by the earthshaking rumble scatter in the air. Kennedy Space Center, Cape Canaveral, Florida.

Space Shuttle *Discovery* Launching. The space shuttle *Discovery* rises from the Launch Pad 39-B at 11:37 a.m. EDT on September 29, 1988. It takes five seconds for the shuttle to clear the 247-foot-high tower and its 100-foot-high lightning rod. Kennedy Space Center, Cape Canaveral, Florida. *© CORBIS*

Space Shuttle *Discovery* Launching. The space shuttle *Discovery* rises from Launch Pad 39-B at 11:37 a.m. EDT on September 29, 1988. Notice that the three main engines of the orbiter are firing but not producing smoke; the blue triangles just below the main engines are called "blue mach diamonds." Kennedy Space Center, Cape Canaveral, Florida. © *Roger Ressmeyer/CORBIS*

Space Shuttle *Discovery* Launching. The space shuttle *Discovery* leaves Launch Pad 39-B at 11:37 a.m. EDT on September 29, 1988. In the first eight seconds into the flight, the shuttle travels only twice it own length but consumes more than a million-and-half pounds of fuel, about half of the shuttle's total fuel supply. Kennedy Space Center, Cape Canaveral, Florida.   © *Roger Ressmeyer/CORBIS*

Space Shuttle *Discovery* Launching. The space shuttle *Discovery* shortly after lift off at 11:37 a.m. EDT on September 29, 1988. About twenty seconds into the flight, the shuttle rolls so the orbiter lies under the external fuel tank and the solid rocket boosters. This maneuver is necessary to reduce aerodynamic stress on the orbiter's wings and tail as Mach 1 is approached. Kennedy Space Center, Cape Canaveral, Florida. © *Roger Ressmeyer/CORBIS*

Space Shuttle *Atlantis* in the Vehicle Assembly Building. The space shuttle *Atlantis* hangs in the Vehicle Assembly Building (VAB), one of the largest buildings in the world, prior to being mated to the rest of the STS stack (the External Tank and the pair of SRBs) in preparation for the twenty-ninth shuttle mission (STS-30), which would launch on May 4, 1989. Kennedy Space Center, Cape Canaveral, Florida. *March 13 1989.*
© *Roger Ressmeyer/CORBIS*

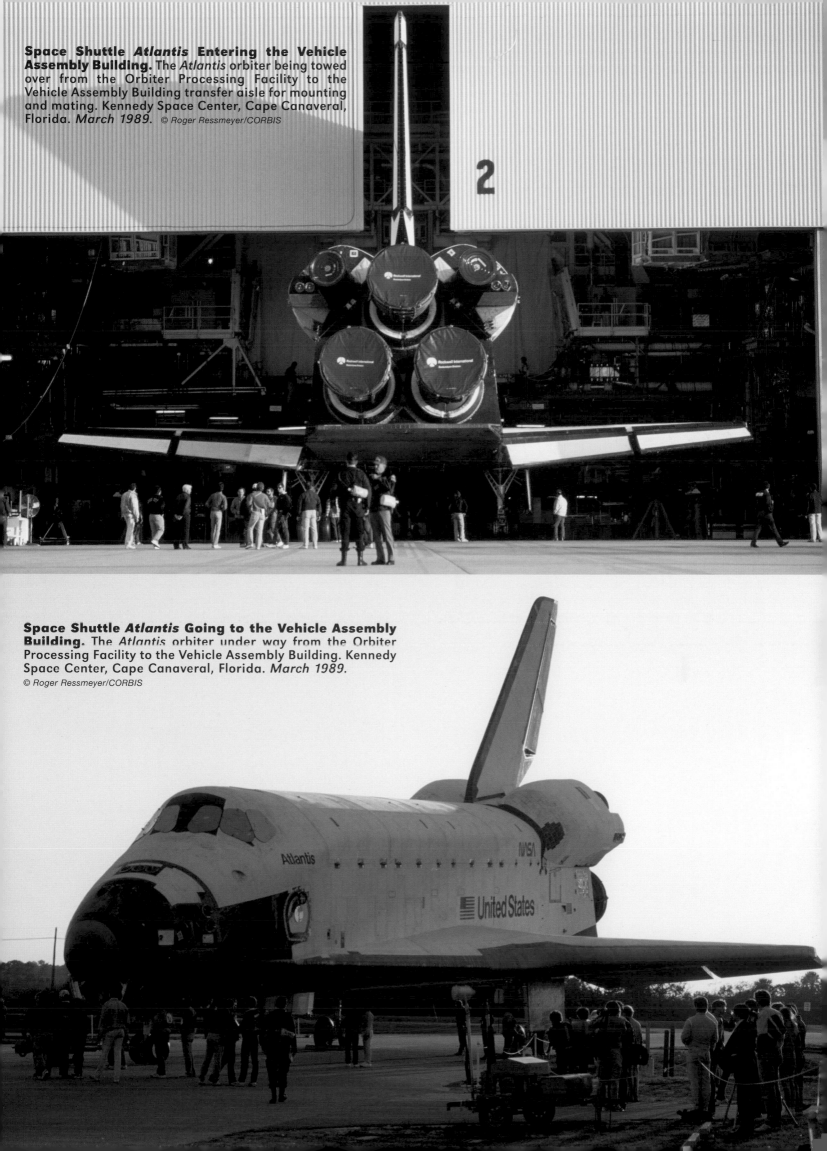

Space Shuttle *Atlantis* Entering the Vehicle Assembly Building. The *Atlantis* orbiter being towed over from the Orbiter Processing Facility to the Vehicle Assembly Building transfer aisle for mounting and mating. Kennedy Space Center, Cape Canaveral, Florida. *March 1989.* © Roger Ressmeyer/CORBIS

Space Shuttle *Atlantis* Going to the Vehicle Assembly Building. The *Atlantis* orbiter under way from the Orbiter Processing Facility to the Vehicle Assembly Building. Kennedy Space Center, Cape Canaveral, Florida. *March 1989.*
© Roger Ressmeyer/CORBIS

Space Shuttle *Discovery* on Launch Pad. The space shuttle *Discovery* sits on Launch Pad 39-B at sunset the evening before its launch on March 13, 1989, for the twenty-eighth shuttle mission (STS-29). Kennedy Space Center, Cape Canaveral, Florida. *March 12 1989.* © *Roger Ressmeyer/CORBIS*

Space Shuttle *Discovery* Launching. The space shuttle *Discovery* blasts off at 9:57 a.m. EST on March 13, 1989, for the twenty-eighth shuttle mission (STS-29), with the primary objective of deploying the third Tracking and Data Relay Satellite (TDRS-4). Kennedy Space Center, Cape Canaveral, Florida. © *Roger Ressmeyer/CORBIS*

Launching _Magellan_. The _Magellan_ probe, the primary payload of the twenty-ninth shuttle mission (STS-30), being deployed from the cargo bay of the space shuttle _Atlantis_. This exploratory spacecraft was successfully launched on a fifteen-month voyage to Venus that would produce a radar map of over seventy percent of that planet's surface. _May 4 1989._

© NASA/Roger Ressmeyer/CORBIS

Space Shuttle *Atlantis* Launch Trail. The ascent trail of the space shuttle *Atlantis* following blast-off at 2:52 a.m. EST on February 28, 1990, for the thirty-fourth shuttle mission (STS-36), dedicated to classified military purposes. The multiple exposure technique that captures the trail of shuttle's ascent also illuminates the night. Kennedy Space Center, Cape Canaveral, Florida. *© Roger Ressmeyer/CORBIS*

Launch of Space Shuttle *Atlantis*. The space shuttle *Atlantis* blasting off at 9:22 a.m. EST on April 5, 1991, for the thirty-ninth shuttle mission (STS-37). Kennedy Space Center, Cape Canaveral, Florida.

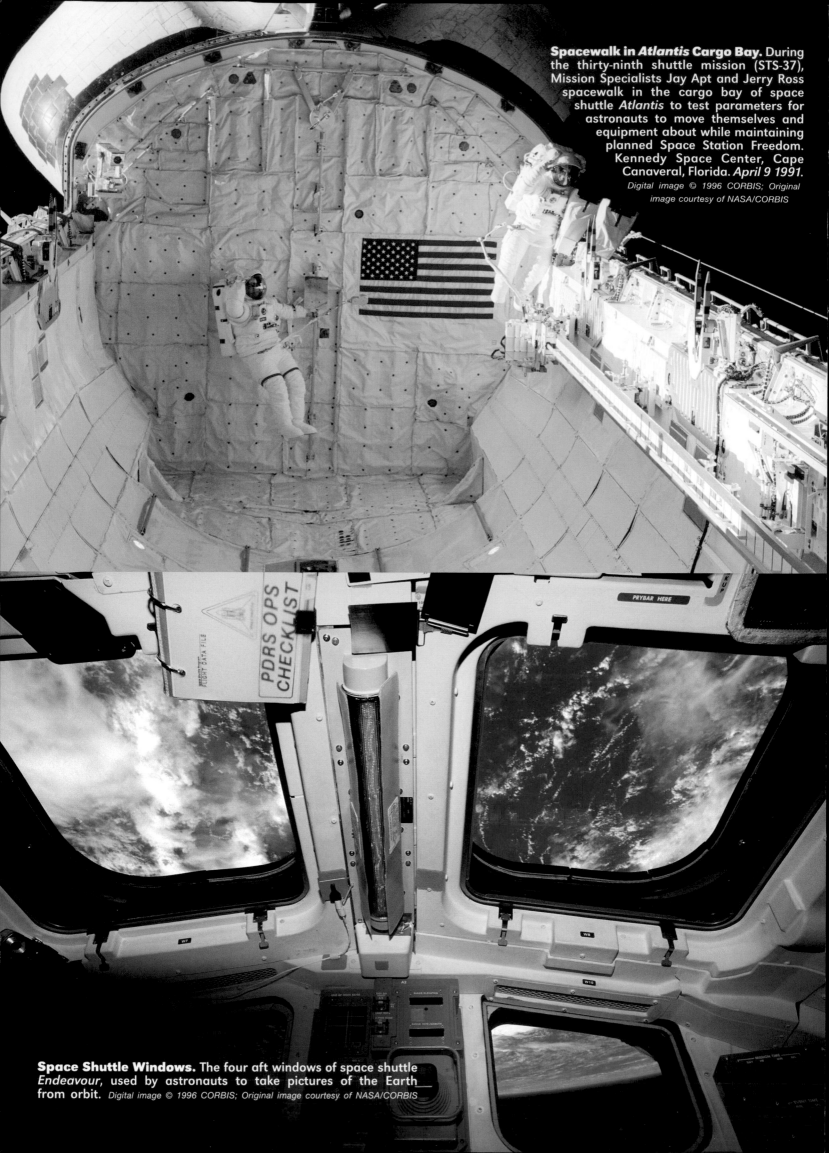

Spacewalk in *Atlantis* Cargo Bay. During the thirty-ninth shuttle mission (STS-37), Mission Specialists Jay Apt and Jerry Ross spacewalk in the cargo bay of space shuttle *Atlantis* to test parameters for astronauts to move themselves and equipment about while maintaining planned Space Station Freedom. Kennedy Space Center, Cape Canaveral, Florida. *April 9 1991.*

Space Shuttle Windows. The four aft windows of space shuttle *Endeavour*, used by astronauts to take pictures of the Earth from orbit.

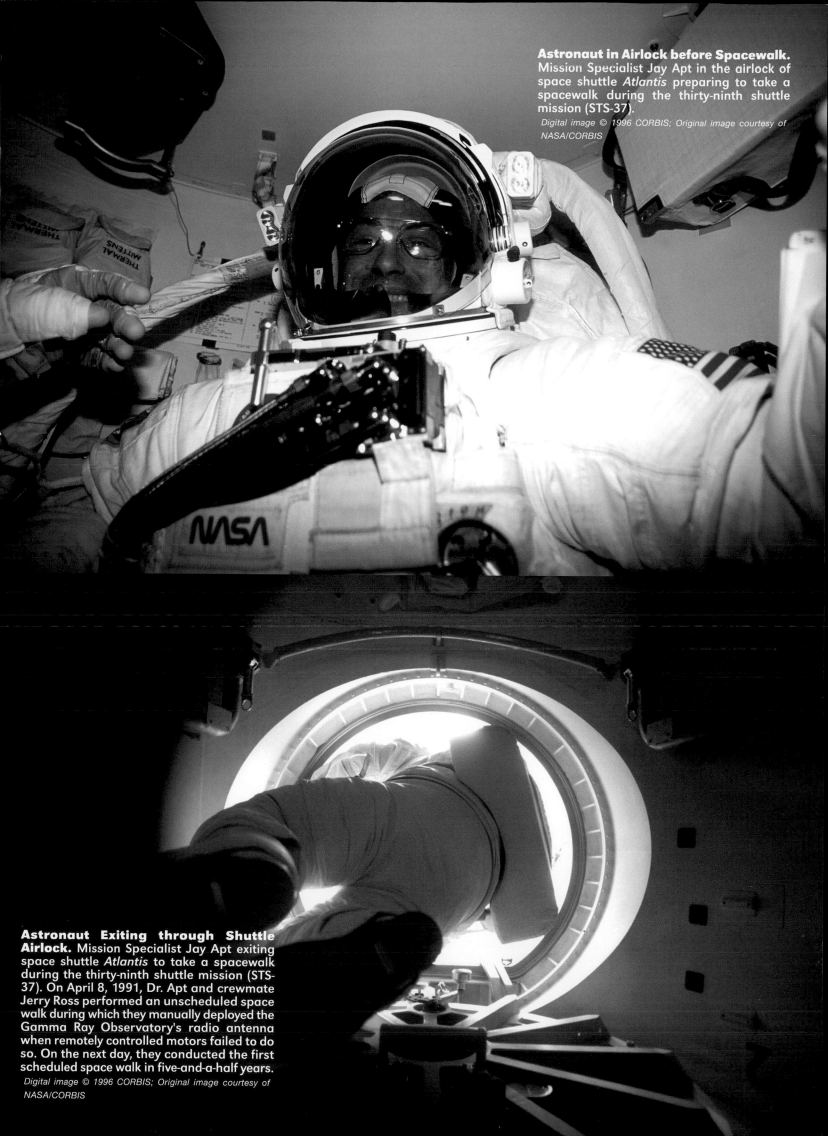

Astronaut in Airlock before Spacewalk. Mission Specialist Jay Apt in the airlock of space shuttle *Atlantis* preparing to take a spacewalk during the thirty-ninth shuttle mission (STS-37).

Astronaut Exiting through Shuttle Airlock. Mission Specialist Jay Apt exiting space shuttle *Atlantis* to take a spacewalk during the thirty-ninth shuttle mission (STS-37). On April 8, 1991, Dr. Apt and crewmate Jerry Ross performed an unscheduled space walk during which they manually deployed the Gamma Ray Observatory's radio antenna when remotely controlled motors failed to do so. On the next day, they conducted the first scheduled space walk in five-and-a-half years.

Crew of Space Shuttle *Atlantis*. The six members of the forty-fourth shuttle mission (STS 44) included: (left to right, front row) Pilot Terence Henricks, Commander Frederick Gregory, and Mission Specialist Story Musgrave; (left to right, back row) Mission Specialist James Voss, Payload Specialist Thomas Hennen, and Mission Specialist Mario Runco. *Atlantis* would travel almost three million miles on its classified STS-44 mission, beginning on November 24, 1991. *July 1991.* © CORBIS

Crew of Space Shuttle *Endeavour*. The seven members of the fiftieth shuttle mission (STS-47), wearing their launch-and-entry suits: (left to right, seated) Mission Specialist Jay Apt and Pilot Curtis Brown; and (left to right, rear) Mission Specialist Jan Davis, Payload Commander Mark Lee (Davis and Lee, the first married couple to fly in space), Commander Robert "Hoot" Gibson, Mission Specialist Mae Jemison (first African-American woman to fly in space), and Payload Specialist Mamoru Mohri (representing the National Space Development Agency of Japan). In the background are the flags of the United States and Japan. STS-47 would conduct a host of Spacelab-Japan materials science experiments in this joint NASA/NASDA mission, beginning on September 12, 1992. Johnson Space Center, Houston, Texas. *June 1992.* © CORBIS

Crew of Space Shuttle *Columbia*. The seven members of the forty-eighth shuttle mission (STS-50) included: (left to right) Mission Specialist Ellen Shulman, Pilot Kenneth Bowersox, Payload Commander Bonnie Dunbar, Commander Richard Richards, Mission Specialist Carl Meade, Payload Specialist Eugene Trinh, and Payload Specialist Lawrence DeLucas. Beginning on June 25, 1992, STS-50 would last 13 days, making it the longest shuttle mission to date. Palmdale, California. *January 1992.* © CORBIS

Crew of Space Shuttle *Endeavour*. The five members of the fifty-third shuttle mission (STS-54), wearing their launch-and-entry suits, pose for their official crew portrait on the flight deck of Johnson Space Center's motion-based shuttle mission simulator: (left to right) Mission Specialist Mario Runco, Commander John Casper, Pilot Donald McMonagle, Mission Specialist Susan Helms, and Mission Specialist Gregory Harbaugh. The primary payload of STS-55, which launched on January 13, 1993, was the fifth Tracking and Data Relay Satellite. *August 1992.* © CORBIS

Crew of Space Shuttle *Endeavour* on Way to Launch. The seven members of the fiftieth shuttle mission (STS-47), wearing their launch-and-entry suits, leave the Kennedy Space Center's Operations and Checkout Building to board a van headed to Launch Complex 39 for the launch of shuttle *Endeavour* on the morning of September 12, 1992. Leading the crew is Commander Robert "Hoot" Gibson (front right). He is followed by Mission Specialist Jay Apt (glasses, front center), Pilot Curtis Brown (front left), Mission Specialist Jan Davis (center left), Payload Commander Mark Lee (center right), Payload Specialist Mamoru Mohri (waving back left), and Mission Specialist Mae Jemison (back right). Kennedy Space Center, Cape Canaveral, Florida.

Digital image © 1996 CORBIS; Original image courtesy of NASA/CORBIS

Crew of Space Shuttle *Endeavour* Perform Microgravity Stunt. Three members of the fiftieth shuttle mission (STS-47) demonstrate the persistence of command structure in microgravity: (top to bottom) Commander Robert "Hoot" Gibson, Pilot Curtis Brown, and Payload Specialist Mamoru Mohri. Earth orbit. *September 1992.* © NASA/*Roger Ressmeyer/CORBIS*

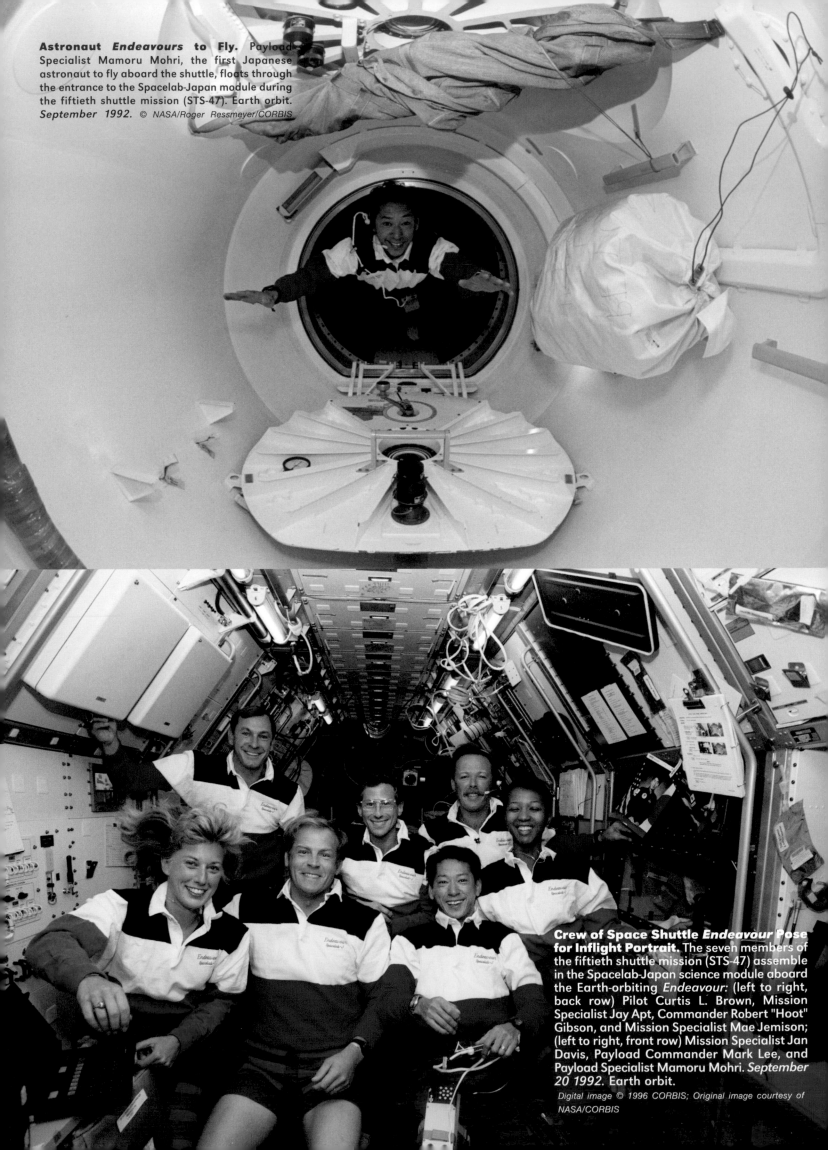

Astronaut _Endeavours_ to Fly. Payload Specialist Mamoru Mohri, the first Japanese astronaut to fly aboard the shuttle, floats through the entrance to the Spacelab-Japan module during the fiftieth shuttle mission (STS-47). Earth orbit. _September 1992._ © _NASA/Roger Ressmeyer/CORBIS_

Crew of Space Shuttle _Endeavour_ Pose for Inflight Portrait. The seven members of the fiftieth shuttle mission (STS-47) assemble in the Spacelab-Japan science module aboard the Earth-orbiting _Endeavour:_ (left to right, back row) Pilot Curtis L. Brown, Mission Specialist Jay Apt, Commander Robert "Hoot" Gibson, and Mission Specialist Mae Jemison; (left to right, front row) Mission Specialist Jan Davis, Payload Commander Mark Lee, and Payload Specialist Mamoru Mohri. _September 20 1992._ Earth orbit.

Digital image © 1996 CORBIS; Original image courtesy of NASA/CORBIS

Space Shuttle *Endeavour* Blasting Off. *Endeavour* blasts off at 10:23 a.m. EDT on September 12, 1992, for its second trip into space (STS-47). In this low-angle shot, all three "blue mach diamonds" are clearly visible beneath the space shuttle main engines. Exhaust plumes trail from the twin booster skirts. The SST is about to begin its roll maneuver. Kennedy Space Center, Cape Canaveral, Florida.

Powering Down Space Shuttle *Endeavour.* On the shuttle's forward flight deck, Commander Robert "Hoot" Gibson (left) and Pilot Curtis Brown power down space shuttle *Endeavour* after landing her at 8:53 a.m. EDT on September 20, 1992, on Runway 33 of Kennedy Space Center. At the completion of the eight days and 126 orbits of the Spacelab-Japan mission, the two STS-47 pilots are running through their checklist of power-down procedures.

Crew of Space Shuttle *Discovery*. The five members of the fifty-second shuttle mission (STS-53), wearing their launch-and-entry suits, pose for their official crew portrait in front of a space shuttle orbiter model at the Johnson Space Center in Houston: (left to right, front) Mission Specialist Guion Bluford, Mission Specialist James Voss; (left to right, back) Commander David Walker, Pilot Robert Cabana, and Mission Specialist Michael Clifford. *September 1992.* © CORBIS

Space Shuttle *Discovery* Blasting Off.
Discovery lifts off from Launch Pad 39-A at 8:42 a.m. EST on December 2, 1992, for the fifty-second shuttle mission (STS-53). Kennedy Space Center, Cape Canaveral, Florida.
© CORBIS

Space Shuttle *Columbia* Launching. The space shuttle *Columbia* blasting off at 10:53 a.m. EST on October 18, 1993, for STS-58 to accomplish the fourth longest mission in U.S. manned space flight. The crew carried out experiments on the adaptability of the human body to weightlessness. Kennedy Space Center, Cape Canaveral, Florida. © *Bettmann/CORBIS*

Space Shuttle *Columbia* on Launch Pad at Night. Floodlights illuminate the *Columbia*, the now veteran craft, at Kennedy Space Center, Cape Canaveral, Florida, for its launch on October 18, 1993. © *CORBIS*

Space Shuttle *Endeavour* on Launch Pad. The space shuttle *Endeavour* sits on Launch Pad 39-B just prior its launch at 4:26 a.m. EST on December 2, 1993, for the fifty-ninth shuttle mission (STS-61). Its high-profile mission was to repair the Hubble Space Telescope. Kennedy Space Center, Cape Canaveral, Florida.
© *Roger Ressmeyer/CORBIS*

Crew of Space Shuttle *Endeavour*. The seven members of (STS-61), suited up before launch: (from left to right) Mission Specialist Claude Nicollier, Pilot Kenneth D. Bowersock, Commander Richard O. Covey, Mission Specialist Thomas D. Akers, Mission Specialist Kathryn C. Thornton, Payload Commander F. Story Musgrave and Mission Specialist Jeffrey A. Hoffman. In their eleven-day flight, the crew set a record of five spacewalks. Johnson Space Center, Houston, Texas. *December 1993.* © Roger Ressmeyter/ CORBIS

Crew of Space Shuttle *Endeavour*. The seven members of the fifty-ninth shuttle mission (STS-61), in casual garb: (top row) Payload Commander F. Story Musgrave, Mission Specialist Jeffrey A. Hoffman, Mission Specialist Kathryn C. Thornton, Mission Specialist Thomas D. Akers, (bottom row) Mission Specialist Claude Nicollier of Switzerland, Pilot Kenneth D. Bowersock and Commander Richard O. Covey. On this mission Musgrave and Hoffman accomplished the second longest spacewalk in U.S. flight history, clocking in at seven hours and fifty minutes. Johnson Space Center, Houston, Texas. *December 1993.* © NASA/Roger Ressmeyer/ CORBIS

Crew of Space Shuttle *Endeavour*. The astronauts of the mission to fix the Hubble Space Telescope pose with their ship in the background. Kennedy Space Center, Cape Canaveral, Florida. *November 4 1993.* © Roger Ressmeyer/ CORBIS

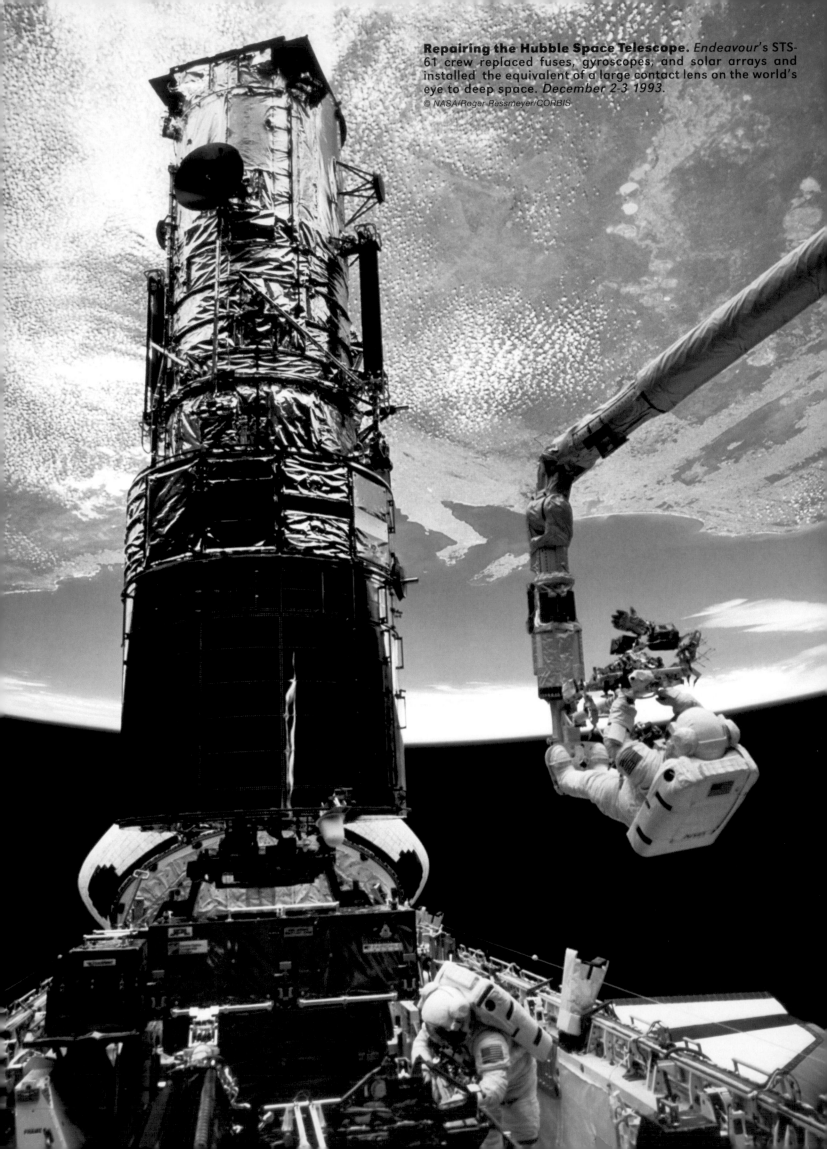

Repairing the Hubble Space Telescope. *Endeavour's* STS-61 crew replaced fuses, gyroscopes, and solar arrays and installed the equivalent of a large contact lens on the world's eye to deep space. *December 2–3 1993.*

An Unearthly Earthly Sight from _Endeavour_. Over Antarctica, the space shuttle views the Aurora Australis. Maneuvering thrusters are being fired. *Digital image ©1996 CORBIS; Original image courtesy of NASA/CORBIS*

Space Shuttle _Columbia_ Over the Libyan Desert. *July 1994. Digital image © 1996 CORBIS; Original image courtesy of NASA/CORBIS*

Space Shuttle *Discovery* Soars Aloft. The space shuttle *Discovery* blasts off Launch Pad 39-B at 6:22 p.m. EST on September 9, 1994. STS-64 is the nineteenth flight for *Discovery*. Kennedy Space Center, Cape Canaveral, Florida.

© CORBIS

Shuttle Astronaut Makes Untethered Spacewalk. *Discovery's* STS-64 Mission Specialists Mark Lee (pictured) and Carl Meade make the first U.S. untethered spacewalk in over a decade.

A View from Space Station *Mir*. The nose of space shuttle *Atlantis* on STS-71 is visible from Russian Space Station *Mir* in the summer of 1995. *Digital image © 1996 CORBIS; Original image courtesy of NASA/CORBIS*

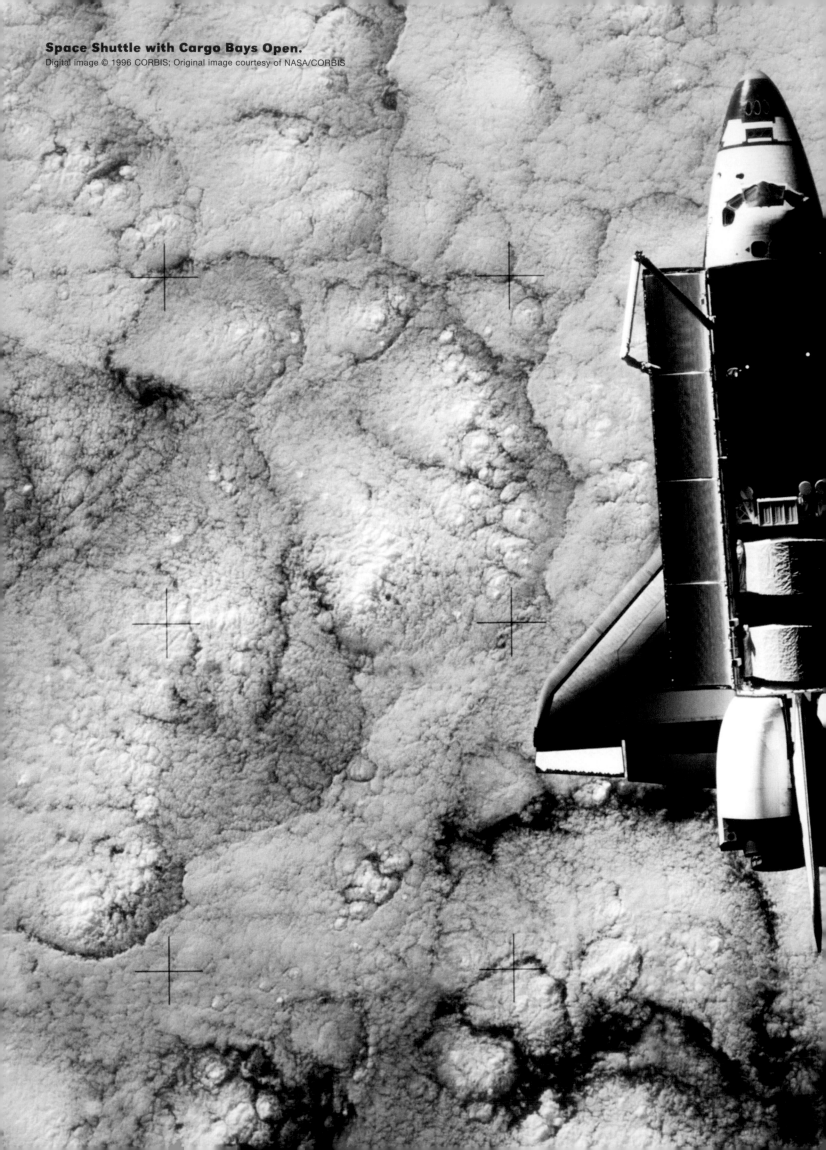

Space Shuttle with Cargo Bays Open.

Here's Looking at You, Kid. Space shuttle *Atlantis* STS-71 Commander Robert L. Gibson looks out a shuttle porthole towards the *Mir*. *Digital image © 1996 CORBIS; Original image courtesy of NASA/COF*

THIS PAGE:
Shuttle *Discovery* Lifts Off. Kennedy Space Center, Cape Canaveral, Florida.
© *Mark M. Lawrence/CORBIS*

OPPOSITE PAGE TOP:
Crew of Space Shuttle *Discovery*. Mission STS-95 crew members are: (front row) Payload Specialist Chiaki Mukai of Japan, Mission Commander Curt Brown; (middle row) Pilot Steve Lindsey, Payload Specialist John H. Glenn; (back row) Mission Specialist Scott Parazynski, Mission Specialist Stephen Robinson and Mission Specialist Pedro Duque. John Glenn was the first American to orbit the earth in 1962. He went back to space October 29, 1998. Kennedy Space Center, Cape Canaveral, Florida. © *AFP/ CORBIS*

OPPOSITE PAGE BOTTOM:
Crew of Space Shuttle *Columbia* Pose. Mission STS-93 crew members are: (from left) Mission Commander Eileen Collins (the first woman shuttle commander), Mission Specialist Steven Hawley, Pilot Jeffrey Ashby, Mission Specialist Michel Tognini (of France), and Mission Specialist Catherine Coleman. They will deploy the Chandra X-Ray Telescope, of which they hold a model. They lifted off July 23, 1999. Kennedy Space Center, Cape Canaveral, Florida. © *Reuters NewMedia Inc./CORBIS*

Space Shuttle Climbs the Pillar of Fire. Kennedy Space Center, Cape Canaveral, Florida. © *Mark M. Lawrence/CORBIS*

Space Shuttle *Atlantis* Heads Out. Mission STS-101 was the Shuttle Program's ninety-eighth flight and the twenty-first for the *Atlantis*. Kennedy Space Center, Cape Canaveral, Florida. *May 19 2000.*
© *Mark M. Lawrence/CORBIS*

The Stars Above, the Earth Below.
© Stocktrek /CORBIS

Greetings from Outer Space.
© Stocktrek/CORBIS

Space Shuttle Climbs to the Heavens. Kennedy Space Center, Cape Canaveral, Florida. © *Mark M. Lawrence/CORBIS*

Space Shuttle *Discovery* Lifts Off. Kennedy Space Center, Cape Canaveral, Florida. © *Mark M. Lawrence/CORBIS*

Space Shuttle *Columbia* Before Its Last Mission. The service structure has just been rolled back from space shuttle *Columbia*, which will spend almost 16 days in orbit on the 113th shuttle mission (STS-107). Kennedy Space Center, Cape Canaveral, Florida.

Old Glory at Half-Mast for the Loss of Space Shuttle *Columbia* and Its Crew. Kennedy Space Center, Cape Canaveral, Florida. © AFP/CORBIS/Peter Muhly

The Saga of Space Exploration and *Discovery* Continues for All. Two young surfers watch the launch of space shuttle *Discovery* on the afternoon of October 29,1998. On this mission (STS-95), U.S. Senator John H. Glenn, who in 1962 became the first American to orbit the Earth, returned to space at the age of 77 for another 134 spins. Cape Canaveral, Florida. © *Reuters NewMedia Inc. /CORBIS*